EACH POEM IS A SUNSET

EACH POEM IS A SUNSET

JOHN WOOD

FIRST EDITION
Printed in the United States of America
ISBN 978-1-956828-00-9

Cataloging Information: 1. Wood, John; 2. Contemporary American Poetry; 3. Each Poem Is a Sunset

Author Photo: Mary Jo Wood

Layout/Design/Cover Concept by Andrew Ayers
using Crimson Text and Arno Pro

Night Rain Press is an imprint of Night Rain Books.

Night Rain Press
PO Box 445
Tillamook, OR 97141

Night.Rain.Press@gmail.com

Contact author John Wood by email at: eastschool0929@gmail.com

for my grandchildren,

Everett and Eleanor,

with love

CONTENTS

THE SUNSET WILL BE YOURS

One Word 3
A Living Book 4
The Sunset Will Be Yours 5
With the Passion of a Poet 6
Inevitable 7
Right Now 8
Do You Know Words? 9
Awake 10

WHERE AM I FROM?

September 13
Seventh Street 14
A Child at Play 15
Grandma 16
Softness 18
Iowa Memories 19
The Kitchen and the Café 20
1959 Chev 21
In all my time in school, 22
You Think You Know Pain 23
Where Am I From? 24
Father in the Mirror 26
Older Brother 28
You Are Sick: Not a Dream 29
A Way Home 30
When One Leaves 31

ON MY WALK

Ocean Going 35
Walking the Ocean Beach 36
Stillness 38
Freeway Travel 39

Wind 40
Why the Wind 42
On My Walk 43
October Rains 44
I Watched the Silence for a Long Time 46
God Lives Here 47
Last Time 48

I BRING COOKIES

God's Painting 53
Tillamook 54
A Door Opening Dog 55
Santa Claus 56
I Bring Cookies 57
The Coming of Morning 58
Why is it 59
The Question 60
To Help 61
A Coat 62
A Hard Life 63
The Scars of Life 64
A Cat's Misstep 66
Somewhere Waiting 67
A New Decade to Live 68
Stepping Again into Your Path 70
Why 71
I Miss Them 72
Seeing You Again No More 73
A Leaving 74
Always With You 75

LOVE AND TIME

Love and Time 79
I Came Because of Me, I Stayed Because of You 80
Mary Jo 82
You May See Love 83
Valentine's Day 84
To Love 85
He Is the Wise Child 86

For Halloween 88
A Last Gift for Peter 89
Left Behind 90
Gone 91
Without You 92

ONE I WILL ALWAYS SEE

One I Will Always See 95
Word Magic 96
A Singer of Songs 98
Try or Not 99
To Escape 100
Unseen Walls 101
The Underworld 102
A Line for Cheese, Another for Death 104
Searching 106

OUR SHARED JOURNEY

A Yesterday Specail One 111
Pile People 112
Revolving Doors 113
Five Rivers Roasters Again 114
Coffee Shop Searching 116
Found By A Few 118
The Final Score 119
Our Shared Journey 120
I Heard You 121
Knowing I Have No Control 122
The Unseen Virus 123
Fog Takes Over the Beach 124
Another Dawn 126
I Made Some Life Stories 127

CHOOSING WHAT TO FIX

Unsure 131
Why or Why Not Resolutions 132
Understanding 133
Choosing What to Fix 134
Push 135

A Broken Signal 136
Cell Phone Washing 137
Computer Ills 138
A Dog's Life 139
Nature and the Cat 140
A Silent Moment 142
When You Listen, You Can Hear 143
The Geese, My Father, and I Walk 144
Nature Plays 145
The Snow 146
Winter Holds On 147
The End of the Path 148

THE PASSING OF TIME

The Passing of Time 153
Forgetting I Might Grow Old 154
Opening Doors 155
This Time I Know 156
To Teach 158
A Word 159
Wide Open Spaces 160
I Find the Quiet Place 162
Want 163
The People I Am 164
Wine and Conversation 165
The Path in, Just Before Dawn Time 166
The Night and I 168
Day and Night 169
The Silence of Time 170
How Many Times: In Time 172

DAY'S END

A Quiet Place 177
Once More: Five River Roasters 178
The Call of Nature 180
Ocean Edge Walk 182
Day's End 183
To Read the Book of Life 184
A Lifetime Walk 186

The Journey of a Life Lived 188
How Did You Live? 189
A Day and a Night 190
In the Words: Life 191

Gratitude 193
About the Author 195

THE SUNSET WILL BE YOURS

One Word

And the words flow,
spoken to me
from that faraway place,
and as I write them down,
I hope they speak to you,
for they are not just my story.
I believe I hear you too,
for when I have spoken, so have you.
When I have heard, so have you,
and when the words flow
they are yours, they are mine,
they are all the words ever spoken.
The many words are one word.

A Living Book

A book of poems
attempts to dream itself
into the eyes of the living.

It has taken the slow path
from a long-time-ago beginning.

Some words
have even heard themselves spoken,
but those and more
still sleep on individual pages.

I, the one
who places the words,
do not hurry the book.

When it's time,
it will be the right time.

Like myself,
the journey in our becoming
comes slowly
but each step taken, worthwhile.

So, book, wait and dream—
all dreams come true.

The Sunset Will Be Yours

I wrote the sunset poem
long before I saw the sunset.
The words had just been there sleeping
until they awoke and came to me.

Each sunset
is a poem or painting
waiting for the artist
or the poet to know it.

Sunsets always surprise my eyes
just before they come alive in me,
and the pen pushes the words
that I hear out of my hand.

The paper saves them,
so if you wish
you can see without your eyes
what mine have seen.

Maybe then you'll be able
to find your own sunset
that, if you are lucky,
will come alive in you.

With the Passion of a Poet

If you cannot hear
the footsteps
of those who came before,

who, then,
will light the torch
so at last
you can see your way?

So, I listened
and heard the words
of a thousand coming.

And they all
whispered my name
and offered words
for me to write.

So it was
that the flame of my soul
flickered,
and then burned
with the passion of a poet.

Inevitable

There is nothing that is inevitable, not even death and taxes. What happens can always be changed by you or another. Some never pay their taxes, and death is just stepping through a door, and our eyes will not let us see what is on the other side. O all right, it is inevitable that all the other writers writing will be brilliant, and yet if there is something put into my path to walk into, I will, and the sun will rise and set.

The dog will bark every time the neighbor goes by. It will rain more than enough in Tillamook. I will drink too much coffee. The crows will gather in the alders. The seasons will tell time for us. The human race seems to never get it right. And tomorrow, I will write another poem. How lucky am I.

Right Now

I let time
stay on the clock.

In the empty space,
I let the river of words flow.

Today,
like a torrent they come.

My pen races
to keep up.

Again, I wonder who sent them
and why they come to me.

It's like a love affair
you can't live without.

The words wash over my mind
and spill into my soul.

A life-giving whispering of words
to sustain the whole of me.

So, I place them on the paper,
a gift given so many times.

As you read them.
you will know why I am still alive.

Do You Know Words?

I lay my pillow
on the pillow of words
that have come to rest
in me.

They are not
always soft—
those are the ones
not meant to let you sleep.

Sometimes the river of words
storms over me,
a maddening, rushing, turbulence
that scares even me.

Then come the ones
so quiet, almost silent—
you feel rather than hear them
as they burrow into your soul.

As long as I am given
each word,
I know
I will live another day.

Awake

I awaken
still in the darkness of the night.

Slowly, I prepare myself
to paint once more
on the canvas of my soul
with another day of my living.

Slowly, slowly
I brush all the years
I have been given.

In this fragile landscape
that is the universe of my beginning,
I begin to glimpse the face of me.

The golden ball of morning
dazzles its lights
on the pathway of my destination.

WHERE AM I FROM?

September

Born in September,
that unsure month
   between
summer's end and
fall's beginning.

I find myself
most times unsure
   between
sunshine and
rain.

And like the weather,
undecided
which way to go.

Seventh Street

A narrow dirty street.
But it was ours.
We owned it.

A war with the enemies across the street
left dirty windows, and Dave
with his head cracked open.

Watering the bees made it a fast race to the house,
and an unhappy mother.

I rolled the boulder over myself,
and Steve was run over by the doctor next door,
but we all recovered when we heard the bell
of the man in the ice cream wagon.

I ran away from home,
all the way to the end of the street,
and mom came home with the police.

I fell in love with the girl across the street,
she moved.
I cried, but a good dirt clod fight
and life went on.

Seventh Street, like any street,
but I was there,
I've gone, but I gained and lost,
and lived on Seventh Street.

A Child at Play

Again, I go
to a long past yesterday,
becoming again
a child at play.

Running in the sand,
leaving small footprints
the waves
wash away.

Buckets of sand
become sandcastles,
rocks and shells,
homeward bound treasures.

Racing waves
to keep my feet dry,
chasing birds
from peaceful perches.

Leaving now,
again an adult
wishing the childhood
I wished away could stay.

Grandma

Small child,
growing with the tall green corn,
the big white house,
and you, Grandma.

Big barn,
hayloft,
and the sky-high swing.

Stair steps,
slow tick grandfather clock,
and the big stone fireplace.

Pump-handle well,
green grass,
and sun hiding trees.

Fence row,
multi-colored peacock,
and the no-top windmill.

A piece of pie,
a chocolate milk shake,
and the food-covered table.

Big dogs,
even bigger horses,
and long, hot summers.

Small child,
growing with the tall green corn,
and the big white house,
and you, Grandma.

Softness

Going by fields of freshly mowed hay,

the smell as sweet as a woman's perfume.

Iowa Memories

Fort Dodge, Iowa born,
but soon left for Oregon,
to wait for father soldier to return.

Later, many summer Iowa visits
and farm life memories made.

A long time ago now,
but I can still see and touch
the large white farmhouse
and hear the corn grow.

The Kitchen and the Café

My grandmother
was the kitchen.
My grandfather
was the café.

She warmed the kitchen
with food and kindness.
He gave the café to me
with conversation and friends.

And both of them,
in their big white farmhouse,
left love for me
to find in every room.

So many years ago now,
only memories for my heart to hold,
but she still warms all my kitchens
and he still leaves me words in every café.

1959 Chev

It had no brakes
   the lights were poor
the seats were torn
   the paint was rusted
the motor clanged
   the muffler banged
held together with glue and
   bailing wire
bald tires and broken glass
   that Chev had a lot of other
good points and it hurt
   to say goodbye.

In all my time in school,

I always wondered,
why there was never a class
in being
a human being.

But then
who would teach it?

And would anyone
pass the class?

You Think You Know Pain

You think you know pain—
be picked last
for every playground game.

Catch but be unable to throw.

Lose your balance
trying anything.

Do nothing that requires two hands.

Many worse off than me,
but as a child.
you only see yourself.

You think you know pain.

Where Am I From?

I am from
the country's center
where tall corn talks
and soybean greens.

I am from
the open spaces of cattle country,
Burma Shave signs
used to live here on roadside edges.

Here, too,
you will find
a famous wall
for free drinking water.

We left the snow of winter
and the sticky sweat of summer
to live in desert dry
by the long river.

War was just down the road
and sailed the world oceans,
but my father came back alive
from a long run across Omaha Beach.

In this new land,
my brothers, sisters, and I
ran free
and the sky always seemed big and blue.

So many of these moments now
seem so far away,
all those many, many days
gone into fast passing years.

My life now lived on the ocean's edge,
near mountains of tall green trees,
cows roaming green, green fields
making milk for famous cheese.

The gifts of a long life given to me—
family and friends found near and far
and all of life
now seems to be where I'm from.

Father in the Mirror

There was a day
when I looked in the mirror
and the same face as always
wasn't there.

This morning
as I prepared to shave myself,
I now saw
my father looking back at me.

Like most people,
I had hoped maybe
time would have left me alone
and all my years added to someone else.

Why I noticed
the change today,
I'm not sure.
More gray hair didn't help though.

Yet, it is still my face,
the same one that lived in my youth.
But now rivers of wrinkles
form miniature valleys here and there.

I'm not really into faces,
not even mine.
I think it's inside
where the real of people lives.

So, I'll just take a moment
and say hi again to dad.
I hardly did
when his face really stood before me.

Then, as I always have,
I'll take my face and the rest of me
and go see what the day has to offer,
and maybe I can leave something good
behind in it too.

Older Brother

Older brother, substitute father,
and the one I always followed behind.

Sometimes you were near,
sometimes far away from me,
but always you were closer.

So many shared days
that too quickly
turned into many passing years.

Two lives so different, I thought.
You to the city and money.
I to the small town
and into the lives of children.

You a traveler, I in one place,
but always, always,
you the brave one I wanted to be.

Not all our moments lived
became as our dreams
as we might have wished.

I only hope
more good than bad
have each of us
left upon the earth and others.

You Are Sick: Not a Dream

This is not
what I would write on any other day,
and if this was truly a dream
I would wake up and be okay.

I am wide awake, though,
as you tell me you are sick.
Liver cancer they tell you
and I cannot fix it by waking up.

You are the youngest
of all the kids in the family—
how strange it feels
that it is not I to be first or second.

It's too early to know yet
how long this path
you're now walking will go
and what the end will look like.

This I know—
I would take it from you
if I had such powers
but I am too weak for this.

So, I'll just be one step behind
and catch you if you fall
and then carry you the rest of the way.

A Way Home

I was going to climb another mountain. This one came with a way home that my brother had told me about.

My brother and I had climbed many mountains together but not this one. I saved this one until he was gone.

Toward the last of his days, he had told me to go to the top of this mountain and I would know where he had gone.

I climbed most of the day but didn't quite get to the top before dark.

I rose early the next morning just as the sun was about to break over the mountain top.

As I reached the top of the mountain, my eyes came on an old wooden door standing open and facing toward the east.

The yellow-gold of the morning sun shone right through the doorway onto my face.

Just as I was about to step through the door, I heard a voice.

Do not come through, brother, it is not your time, but I will wait for you.

I left the mountain top with the warm sun on my back and his words in my heart.

When One Leaves

I lay into the music
and an afternoon cup of coffee,
two deaths lay heavy
on mind and heart.

No one's lifetime line is set,
as somewhere on it,
we begin to realize
it's only the moment we have.

When those close leave,
sometimes a surprise, sometimes not,
for me the empty space is large,
the loss felt as a heavy missing.

An old age given
only means more are gone,
the emptiness grows larger
for those no longer seen.

Memories of those gone
come and go,
following us
into today and tomorrow.

I try now
to enjoy each day in its coming.
Even if we don't want it to be so,
this one may be the last one given.

ON MY WALK

Ocean Going

The waves
left a treasure
upon the sand.

I picked it up
on my walk this morning
going nowhere.

It rests in my pocket.
I'll take it out as
a reminder of how lucky I am.

Like most,
my first sight of the ocean,
I'll always remember.

And when I return,
the gift of this place
is no less than the first time.

All should have these moments—
places that open doors
to feeling.

Walking the Ocean Beach

I follow footsteps that
make a path though ocean edge sand.

Each time I do this,
I wonder about the life stories—
who put passings here
for me to see?

Did they care that someone
following behind them
might want to know
something of them?

Like the never-ending waves
people come to see,
something bigger than themselves,
and maybe even to feel small.

I often come
just for the wonder of it.

The sand seems not to mind
if I leave behind
some of what the world
has made hard.

The ocean waves have taken
much from many people.

Like a setting free,

one can leave here
having written life story
that is brand new.

I do this each time
I go to the beach,
becoming a better person
when I leave, I hope.

Stillness

Nothing moves,
afraid to break the stillness.

How can the world
move across the universe
and not cause a mighty wind
that would carry us all away?

Even the birds
have hidden themselves away.

Finally, I move,
pushing hard against the nothing,
needing the pause of the world
to know that I am here.

Freeway Travel

I am on the green grass hill
watching the waters of the Columbia
traveling by
on their forever journey.

Noise of cars and trucks
reaches my ears from freeway traffic.
Do any ever see
the beauty through which they pass?

So fast in the hurry of life,
coming from or going to,
they seem not to notice
the wonder of the day.

Spring-green covered mountains,
vast blue sky,
a gentle breeze
that ripples the river.

Wind

The wind blows cold,
north by east
winter comes again,
least we think
we know the weather rules.

Inside and warm,
like the bear,
we grow a heavy coat
before going outdoors.

Tomorrow still there, wind,
beach walking for only a few,
I need not go out.

I sometimes wonder
from where comes the wind
and where does it go?

Why hot or cold,
hard or gentle,
here or there—
another God toy?

Maybe for those who write,
poem-making material,
and I do like the wind.

If not the wind,
rain,
too much already this year.

Why the Wind

In the darkness,
the wind blows sideways.

Unseen,
yet its voice
fills any empty space
before it reaches my hearing.

There is a knowing
it is cold,
even when I am inside
in the warm.

Do you ever ask,
as I do,
from where does the wind come,
and why the starting and stopping?

I've asked
the wind
and have received no answer.

On My Walk

Each step
finds a rhythm,
a flow
carries me along
on my walk.

Sometimes others
are there also,
moving
beside me.

On the days
the sun warms our backs,
I come alive.

With another,
words pass the time.
Yet I need none,
for all around,
I can hear the world.

I need not
measure distance traveled.
This journey is for the body.
And for moving.

October Rains

Fall comes,
October rains.

Soon everything is wet,
many become inside people.

Puddles become ponds,
empty streams, rivers again.

Flowers lay flat,
roads become car skating rinks.

Even in the rain unseen,
rain makes music on the roof.

Would we could share
with California's wildfires.

They may have forgotten
last winter's floods.

I care not unless a few days rain
becomes months.

In Tillamook, I know it can.
Ask Lewis and Clark.

I like the song
that rain sings

if its music
soon stops.

I Watched the Silence for a Long Time

Here in this spot,
  it is a deep dark.

I found this silence more pleasing,
  seeming so long to have been here.

I would hope if you pass this way,
  you would not come too close.

This silence, I think,
  is meant to stay longer than you or me.

God Lives Here

I used to sit in churches
listening to others speaking of God,
saying that this was his house.

I do believe God is there,
and in everyone who enters.
But for me God lives in a world She made.

So, I walk among the trees of the forest,
walk the beach and touch the ocean's waters,
and I climb to the top of small mountains.

I sit and whisper back to the flowing stream
and yell at the roaring river
and travel by the light of the full moon.

And whether I am with friends,
or alone in the silence,
I find He lives in all those places, too.

The God I know
lives everywhere,
and deep in my soul.

Last Time

When is the last time
you
offered your hand to another?

When is the last time
you
opened the door to yourself,
letting another in?

When is the last time
you
played in the ocean
and realized, again, how small you are?

When is the last time
you
watched the sunrise as it kissed the sky,
knowing then how lucky you were
to have another day?

When was the last time
you
said thank you
and meant it?

When is the last time
you
listened to the music
and sang?

When is the last time
you
took a breath
and felt alive?

When is the last time
you
were loved and loved back?

When is the last time
you
hoped this would not be the last time?

I BRING COOKIES

God's Painting

The sun rises,
setting the mountain tops on fire,
the colors so bright
they burn my eyes.
It's in the moments like this
that it's easy
to believe in God.

Tillamook

From where the ocean lives
fed by five rivers,
the trees grow tall and green,
and the cows mow cheese.

A Door Opening Dog

I let the dog out again.
In a few minutes,
I'll let him back in again.

I'm not sure
how many times
I have wished
he could learn
how to open the door.

Santa Claus

Santa Claus
came again last night,
at least for the younger ones.

Would it seem strange to you
if I told you
that I still look for him too?

I Bring Cookies

I bring cookies
and sometimes something else,
as if when you eat them,
you will be given a moment
to forget all those things best forgotten.
I know,
they do little,
but sometimes they help bring
three or four bites of happiness.

The Coming of Morning

I sit at the window,
watching the coming
of the morning sun.
Sandy refills my coffee cup.

Sax music
softly fills the air
and my ears.

Early morning, others enter
to find a quiet moment
before the rush of the day.

I think of
friends and enemies
I cannot see.

So much
remembering.

Some are leaving now.
They are now and always
along with me in these thoughts,
this me of this moment.

Soon, in my own leaving,
the moment gone,
hopefully into another
with so much found.

Why is it

so many people ask the question
and then don't believe the answer?

The Question

How do we know
the beginning or ending
of who we are to become?

Is a lifetime
only a searching of one's self?

What of all the others—
do they know why they came?

I believe time
only is given
so that we might find each other.

Those who come to us,
remind us who we are
and light the paths we walk.

Is there an answer
to all we want to know?

Or could it be
the only answer we need
is that we took time to ask why?

To Help

It's much easier to help
  someone up
    than hold them down.

A Coat

Homeless and cold,
I could tell for him
life was a struggle.

Michelle the waitress and I,
having a short conversation,
when the unknown homeless man
entered into her thoughts and words.

The coat I'm wearing, she said
is a man's coat and I should give it to him.

As I was given the gift of watching,
Michelle took off her coat,
walked to him,
handed him the coat, and said,
This should keep you warmer.

He took the coat.
On another morning given to me,
I saw Michelle once more.
She wore a different coat.

How wonderful might life be
if everyone
just gave another person
a coat.

A Hard Life

It is a hard life
he has made.

Each morning over coffee,
he tells me his pains.

I hate my job
another town would be better.

Going to work all the time
yet, I have no money,

I have a few things,
most I don't want.

The things I want,
I cannot get.

He drinks
another cup of coffee.

It is sad, for I think,
this will be the best part of his day.

The Scars of Life

To be alive at all,
is to have scars.
Alive with scars.
The scars of life are many
for everyone, I think.

Many, if not most, of mine
are self-inflicted.

Yet, on most days
I can still see beyond the scars,
and with the coming of a new sunrise,
I get to start over.

Even in these hard times,
Zoom gives me friends
to reach out and touch,
if only from a distance.

Many of the scars of mine
lay waiting in my memories.
Someone wakes in me again,
lest I forget they are there.

Most times scars hurt less
than the first time.

Maybe because newer ones
have come close and taken their places.

Age seems not to have lessened
the pain of a new scar,
yet maybe we would forget how to feel
if we were not scarred upon once in a while.

I have been lucky enough
to be able to help others along the way,
Should this not be a major part of life,
easing away the scars of others?

Another moment of no scars given,
reminds me of all the gifts of life.

Today I walked in the sun
and laid a worry aside.

I am here.
For now, it is enough.

A Cat's Misstep

I could only watch from my car window,
as across the road you ran,
but not fast enough to miss an oncoming car.

Almost a near miss, but you were hit.
A tire found your backside and legs.
New pain for a family already wounded by loss.

Off the road, into the bushes you went,
how I don't know.
I searched for you, but you were gone.

The car driver returned,
sorry, but nothing could be done.
She left, also hurting.

I heard later you were alive,
then I heard a different story.
I did not want to ask which was true.

Somewhere Waiting

after Walt Whitman

I stop somewhere waiting for you,
yet I was there
a thousand somedays ago,
and you have not come.

I thought I knew you well,
and I still hear your voice every day,
but now it's turned into only a whisper.

I stop somewhere waiting for you.
Now, I wait for the sun to rise.
I opened the letter and read.
It says you will not come.

A New Decade to Live

Patches of blue sky
play catch
with the fast-moving clouds.

Winter still,
but it seems it is not so,
as fifty degrees
warms the day.

Even the breeze
sleeps.

The days
have counted themselves
almost to the end
of another year.

A day or two
will bring the beginning
of another decade.

Some that I knew
decided life was too hard,
or maybe
they just needed a change.

They join those I already miss.
Some losses
seem to hurt more than others.

Yet, there is the gift
of those who are still close to me.

So, I still
celebrate each day I am given,
even the really hard ones.

I hope I will live each one
as I wish to,
and each of my wishes
comes true.

And when each one
returns to me
on the long river
of all my memories,

I will know
each day I lived
was one
I was supposed to have lived.

Stepping Again into Your Path

for Lana Ayers

I knew you
when first our eyes met

as if we had traveled together
the journey of many lifetimes.

Our words mingled
in conversations and groups.

Words seem never enough
to say what a gift you became to me.

A sharing of yourself,
even some of the hard parts.

A helping hand
through many of life's stumbles.

An ear and a heart, I think, to gather up
and hold many of my weaknesses.

Few have I found
who accepts one with so many faults.

I hope our shared journey
has many more miles in this life.

You know even when it ends,
I will still have you with me.

Why

Why some died
and others lived?

I don't ask why anymore.

I seem to have enough tears
for both.

I Miss Them

A long life
  has given me
    much.

Yet, many have I known
  are gone.
    I miss them.

I seem to know,
  from deep in my soul,
    they are not really gone.

They are just
  in another place
    unseen by my eyes.

I remember.
  I see them often
    in my memories.

Sometimes
  it is not enough
    and I hurt.

Seeing You Again No More

Again, as I studied
the swirling of life
at the bottom of my watering bucket
that night, thoughts of you came again—
I saw your life becoming smaller and smaller,
and soon, far, far too soon,
it would be no more.

A Leaving

Time
had become almost forever
when I was told
my emptiness
would never again
be quite filled.

For you
had left this place
of living
in which
I still walk.

I was not ready
for your leaving
but maybe
this you already knew
and left
on your own time,
never
to be replaced.

Some
cannot be,
and
a forever hole
there is
in me
where you were.

Always With You

Way, way before the beginning,
as we stood in the shadow of God
waiting for Him to send us off,
I must have known you then.

The life cycle that our lives travel
leaves soul marks of always-together-light
so you and I and the others of us
do not falter from our chosen paths.

I realize I am slow
as I search for the pieces of me,
still many to be found
before the wholeness of me is complete.

Yet you wait, your hand outstretched
taking my hand gently yet firmly,
so that I do not falter or fall
as I follow you through each lifetime.

You have been friend and family,
guide, mentor, leader, and lover to me,
through each and all our living journeys
that will bring us closer and closer to Her.

Even when I could not see you,
I felt you in my heart,
and soon I will open the door to your soul,
step through, and stay with you forever.

LOVE AND TIME

Love and Time

There is nothing more precious
than love and time.

How lucky are you and I
that we have shared those two things
now for forty years.

So many roads of life one might follow,
yet the star of magic
brought the two of us together
those many years ago.

Through so many hills and valleys
did our shared road travel,
you beside me.

Then came a child,
and in just a moment, it seemed,
a wife for him
and two wonderful grandchildren for us.

So many others have touched our lives,
helping to paint the life picture
that we were, we are, and we will become.

May many more days together follow this one,
and may our river of love
takes us gently
into the always and forever.

I Came Because of Me,
I Stayed Because of You

When it was hard,
you made it easier.

When I was down,
you lifted me up.

When I had no answer,
you shared yours.

I came because of me,
I stayed because of you.

When the days were long,
you helped me through.

In the moments of losing,
you made me feel like a winner.

When I struggled with work,
you played with me.

I came because of me,
I stayed because of you.

When I cried,
you showed me how to laugh.

When I felt old,

you made me feel young again.

When many years had passed,
you made them seem like only a moment.

I came because of me,
I stayed because of you.

Mary Jo

In you
came my greatest love
that only grows
with each season of life.

A gift
I cannot measure,
as through the hard and the easy
we held each other up.

A gift of a wonderful son
you gave to us,
a light that reflects you
back to me always.

I can only ask
for many more years to share
with you, the light of love
leading the way.

You May See Love

You may see love in many windows,
but all love needs a door
through which to pass
and be received.

Valentine's Day

I bought flowers
to mark the day.
I seem to find little love
in things.

Would candy or a card
mean more?
Feelings, I think, are
sometimes hard to say.

Some songs,
a soft touch,
at least for me,
hold more meaning.

I tried my best
with some success,
maybe I should
not ask for more.

And I know
love is still there
long after flowers
or even I am gone.

To Love

I would love you
with the whole of me
but I think
that would require
for me to love
a little bit of myself.

He Is the Wise Child

He is
the wise child.
So often I feel
he has given me more
that I could ever give in return.

A life model
many and I
would be wise to follow.
In words and deeds,
he lifts up.

As a father
I would show him the way,
yet most often it seems
I follow
him.

This journey shared,
even when we take
different paths,
seems only to make me better,
and his becoming is a celebration.

So fast has time
made the small him a memory.
He has become a grown-up
so much faster
then I.

He touches the world
with a gentle heart,
a make-change spirit,
living worldwide dreams,
seeing the best in many and me.

His vision,
sometimes hard for me to see,
yet always was he willing
to help me
find mine.

Now living
in the body of a young man,
we walk together, yet apart more.
I watch and rejoice
in his becoming himself.

He is
the wise child.
So often I feel
he has given me more
then I could ever give in return.

For Halloween

Another chance is given
for grandchildren to tire grandparents.

You are five and three now,
almost unfair to us who are old,
unable to run as fast as time anymore.

Again, your bright faces
will shine with our coming.

Few gifts of life
can touch me now with more wonder
than when family comes close.

Ghosts and goblins,
skeletons and jack-o-lanterns,
mixing fear and fun in the night.

Costumed children doorbell ringing
with trick or treat voices heard
on lighted doorsteps and doorways.

Another holiday moment
given over to children's excitement.

A Last Gift for Peter

Did you know
that you had given to me
one of the greatest gifts?
For you brought the family together.

Spread far apart across the country,
seldom have we been able
to find a way
for all of us to gather.

For now, I will carry the light of you
to the dawning of each new day
and with each beat of my heart.

Not a way you would have chosen, I know,
but sometimes things happen in life
without telling us the way of it
or giving us a choice.

So, celebrate the next moment
on the new path,
wherever that takes you,
as I thank you for a last gift given.

Left Behind

Could you say my name again,
and just one more time
look into my eyes and smile?
I know sometimes
we are not given many moments together
and, oh, how it hurts
when you're the one left behind.

Gone

The special times
go much faster.

Today
went into yesterday,
as it always seems to do.

And like that, today now gone,
so are you.

And as hard as I try
I have not found a way
to get either one back.

Without You

A short time
can be a long, long time
without you in it.

ONE I WILL ALWAYS SEE

One I Will Always See

I stood there
until I couldn't see her anymore.
It was then I realized
I would see her forever.

Word Magic

Some people's words
are magic
and they grab hold me of
and never let go.

In the hearing or reading,
I feel them
with the whole of me
and that feeling stays forever.

Each, I know,
has their own talent,
even if it's sometimes hard
for them to see or find it.

We need everyone's talents
but the music maker,
the artist, the author,
and the poet seem to give me more.

I think it is
that each of these people
make me feel
to the point of all that is beyond me.

Each of these people
seem to know me,
even when they don't—
a knowing that is unseen.

I search these people out,
although some seem to find me.
Either way and each time it happens,
I know why there is life.

A Singer of Songs

The notes, rhythms, and words
become the world of your song.

I listen and take it in.
Even if you and your song
are unknown to me,
I know you now.

You come
like a gentle breeze.
Inside, I feel your soft touch.

I paint pictures with my hearing
and hang them next to the door
to my soul.

And in hurting moments,
I will find your voice once more.

Try or Not

Is to try
and fail
the same
as failing to try?

I know it is not true,
for I have not tried
and the failure
has buried me.

To Escape

I still wonder
how you escaped
that terrible childhood world
and became the gift to me
you are.

You've become a mirror
that when I look in,
I will be like you
and escape
myself.

Unseen Walls

Have you ever noticed
it is the walls you can't see
that are the hardest ones
to get over?

I do hope
you are not like me
and build
way too many of them.

The strange thing for me, though,
is that I discovered
that the walls I build
are not to keep others out
but to keep me in.

The walls you can't see
seem harder to knock down,
or maybe the problem is
I never learned how.

The Underworld

They are the homeless,
those who are alone.

They pass
seen but not seen,
known but unknown.

Faces
that tell stories
no one wants to read.

They are alive
but not living.

Most and I
do nothing for them,
but maybe wish often
they weren't there.

Can the world be changed?
If we could
would we?

We don't even
want to be reminded
the next homeless person you see
could be you.

Maybe the first step
for any of us
is to see them.

A Line for Cheese, Another for Death

The cheese factory line grows longer.
Summertime has arrived
and still pandemic numbers rule.

The highway empties cars
into the large parking lot.
Many out-of-staters now
think traveling is safer.

I travel now, too,
not for pleasure.
Being old seems to bring more dying.

Many people go through the factory door,
yet the line still seems to grow.

Peter, soon, and Sam, already.
Maybe one got his wish,
the other fights for life
with all the strength he has left.

I ask again the why of life.
Some say they have all the answers.
I seem to have none.

Strange how hard we search
for what we don't have.

Lunchtime,
the tables outside the cheese factory
fill quickly
with hungry tourists.

The plane for my travels
will come soon.
I go to celebrate two lives
gone before they were ready.

4165 is the cheese factory address.
I wonder if anyone notices it.

Searching

I hope one day
to step out of my own shadow.

A need is there
to ease past
the self-made road blocks.

I look for the one
I am supposed to be,
maybe not even
asking the why of it.

Time has passed
and left me many moments
to find the treasure
I know must be there.

The road has been long,
with many blind corners
that hid the unexpected.

Beautiful people and places
have laid themselves before me.

Too often,
I have lost my way.

I used to call them wrong turns,
but now I think
they were only roads to take
on which I would learn another lesson.

And even in the hardest of times,
someone came
to help me find my way again.

So, on I go,
each foot making another step.

There is a me out there
that will someday come
and stand before me
and say
I am the one you were looking for.

OUR SHARED JOURNEY

A Yesterday Special One

for Linda Shuford

Miles can seem like
a very far distance.

Yet, in the deep silence
when I am alone
I can still bring you close.

For you are a bright star in my nights
and bright sunlight
in all my blue sky days.

And when I swim
in my river of love,
you are at my side.

In my big book
of many memories,
you wait on the first page
for me to see you again.

And I wait
for the the next tomorrow
when my eyes
again see you coming.

Pile People

We who live in piles
want to believe we are organized.
We're not.

We may have a vague idea
of what is in our piles
and the location
of those really important papers.

Some may not even enter a room—
falling piles may be dangerous.

Sometimes, to the surprise of many,
we can run our fingers through a pile
and find just what we need,
just like we knew where in the pile it was.

I tried a few times to be organized,
putting each thing in its place.
Within a week, once more a mess.

Thank you, organized friend,
many times you saved my life.

I can only hope I'm good
at something else and that you
will still come see me.

Just look under the largest pile.

Revolving Doors

To be honest, I do not like revolving doors. They never seemed to turn at a standard speed, and with my extreme lack of coordination, either I, my suitcase, or worst of all, another person, gets stuck in the door. I realize the problems are usually solved quickly, but for a few moments, panic and anger push themselves upon me. Is this why I live in a small town where there are few or no revolving doors?

Every time I go through a revolving door, I'm sure something bad is going to happen, and I always believe everyone around me stops just to see if I'm going to make it through the door. Have you ever had the look from someone, you know the look that says, *let's wait until he goes through,* or *let's hurry and get through before he goes,* or the worst, *I'm already late for my plane and this klutz shows up?*

I realize none of my revolving door problems have been life threatening. God forbid they ever put anyone in the hospital, I think I'd stay home sick.

A thousand stories I could tell you, but maybe I should have written about my coffee cup that has written on it *just two pages away from greatness,* and I've never gotten stuck in a coffee cup.

Five Rivers Roasters Again

I ease through the door.
I have come here enough
that they know my name
and the kind of coffee I drink.

The wall speaker sings
many songs I know
and I relax into them
and listen for words to come.

Most times easy here.
Summer can bring too many,
but I can run away
and come back another time.

They let me have time.
Sometimes I need more than others.
The fan blows gently
and poems are pushed my way.

Most times, I can slow down.
Others here living their own lives.
I am left alone
except for a surprise—friends coming in.

A simple lunch found here, too,
and with a refilled coffee cup,
I let the time go by
without wondering how long it's been.

When I am ready, I leave
knowing I will return.
A moment or two needed
by all and I.

The world and life,
a little easier to take
having been touched
by Five Rivers Roasters.

Coffee Shop Searching

As I drive,
the tires sing
on the wet roads.

As I go along,
I watch the raindrops
making patterns
in the already-made puddles.

One after another,
the drops hit,
then from the centers
expand in circles to the edges.

The clouds hang low,
moving along on unseen winds,
taking shortcuts
through the mountain valleys.

Along with many others,
I find the coffee shop.
A cup of coffee and words
share my time.

Conversations that are not mine
become background noise
that I don't hear when I write.

The weekend,
even on a wet cold day,
brings people here,
an escape from the rainy day.

A young child
joins me at the counter.
We have a conversation about trucks
until his mother returns with hot chocolate.

Enough coffee drank,
I follow others toward the door.
Then refinding the road,
I turn towards home.

Found By A Few

for Neal Lemery

Blown far afield from life,
I am held together
by ones like Neal
who came to share my path.

Such a strange journey for me,
as if in the dark shadows
searching always for self,
unable to see me or my place.

A few, like Neal,
seem not to give up on me,
even as I could never
give enough in return.

Giving more to me
than he will ever know,
even after years of friendship,
he is a model hard to follow.

I hope one day in our shared time,
he will know I know how much
walking together in this life
has meant to me.

The Final Score

Is golf
just a game?
I ask this question
as I share the day with friends.

Or is it so much more—
a few moments to look beyond
the hitting of a ball towards a hole
that takes a long time to reach?

A search too, I think,
for something in us.

A hope for perfection,
with a knowing deep inside
we will never find it.

Yet again, given a remembering
of the value of friendship
in the struggles of life or a game.

And as the day fades into memories,
the score that counts
was not on a card
thrown away when we were finished.

Our Shared Journey

Time and so many yesterdays
have taken themselves behind us,
yet always, yes always,
you are close.

Our shared journey
takes me far beyond myself
and you make the whole of me
remember how to shine.

As our steps, then and now
shared the same path,
you were and are
a bright light I can follow.

So, with each chapter of our life stories,
I take you with me,
far into tomorrow
and the always of us.

I Heard You

I called.
You did not answer,
but I did not mind,
for I heard you anyway,
in all the words
you had spoken to me before.

Knowing I Have No Control

I name again
my brothers and sisters:
David, Stephen, Gretchen,
Susan, and Peter.

Many years
given to all of us.
Life, I think, gave more
than took away.

I look into my memory,
placing close again each of you,
an always thing,
or so I want it to be.

None of us
have tomorrow for sure.
Nothing can make it easier, though,
when one leaves.

The Unseen Virus

I can almost hear
the unseen virus
tapping on my window.

As I look outside again,
I remember I can't go there
without my mask.

The sky is still blue.
The trees are still green
and ocean tides still rise.

Yet the television speaks at me—
Don't go out. Don't go out.
Death will become your new best friend.

Now, I read and write,
but now it's a have to
or I will no longer be sane.

I zoom with you,
but it seems too long without touch.
Are you really still alive?

Even the alone I used to love so much
now has made me into my worst fear—
I have become nothing to the world.

Fog Takes Over the Beach

The fog rolls up the beach
and covers me in dampness
as I walk the edge
of the tide line.

The waves' song
sings in my ears
as my steps are gathered up
by the wet sand.

Today it can be
only my memories
that can see
the far edge of the ocean.

Unseen by my eyes,
a gull's call
filters through the mist
to my ears.

If others are with me,
they are not in my knowing,
as the gray makes distance
not very far.

I have today
come alone
and other people
are not one of my needs.

I lay time aside,
as well as where I am going.
In these moments
I rest.

Taking myself away from myself,
life now only a breath,
feeling only the moments
as they come and go.

These journeys
place my life first
until the world again
calls my name.

Another Dawn

I took the time
to watch the coming
of the dawn
as it crested the hill.

Each morning different than the rest.
For the sun, and I, too.
Yet, always beautiful
for I was alive to see it.

I Made Some Life Stories

The motorcycle rumbles by
carrying a helmet—
another adventure of life
I did not try.

Many roads traveled.
Much country touched my eyes.
I left a smile
as many places as I could.

I gave my name away
to a few friendly folks,
paused in the middle of nature
trying to feel all the life living there.

I walked trails to nowhere.
A few mountaintops felt my feet.
I gave some nights
to lakes and rivers.

I gave my heart away
more than once.
Once it left
and never came back.

Many life stories lived,
not many worth reading,
but a few people I held onto
who made all of life worthwhile.

CHOOSING WHAT TO FIX

Unsure

I wonder why you wonder.

Will the words
push me over some unwanted edge?

If that is a worry,
lay it aside.
Words pushed me over the edge
a long time ago.

Why or Why Not Resolutions

Resolutions are not for me. How many people do I hear make them, but even before they are out of the mouths, they break them? I think they're supposed to help people, but why should we announce what's wrong with us or make a list of things we should do to fix ourselves? Why, too, is it only once a year on January first? If one feels they have something they need to change, why not just start on that right away? I realize some just make a game out of saying resolutions, that they've lost before they began.

Yet, go ahead and make resolutions if you feel the need. I'll support you and celebrate with you if you lose the fifty pounds and get to Boston or New York. Actually, I think I don't make resolutions because then I'd have to write a book telling everyone about the five thousand two hundred and forty-six failed resolutions, and then what would I have left to do the next year?

Understanding

I have failed
to understand many people
and what they do.

Yet, by far the hardest for me
is to understand
what I do or don't do.

Choosing What to Fix

The list of what needs fixing
is never ending.
It was given to us
at the time of our birth.

Did we choose life
so that in the seeing of ourselves
we would know
what *not perfect* could be?

Can that place of *perfect*
be found again,
or is the journey of looking for it
the reason we became human?

Could it be that you and I and all
are already perfect
and all that needs fixing
is the knowing of it?

Push

Sometimes
I push really, really hard
only to discover
I'm pushing in the wrong direction.

So,
I turn around,
and push really, really hard
the other way.

A Broken Signal

The signal light goes off.
People again have to learn
how to share the four-way.
A stop and go, one after another.

This small problem
sets me to thinking again
that to share and give way
really should not be hard.

Why not in all things
a giving and taking,
a looking out after your fellow man?
In all things, the easy and the hard.

Like our heart does on its own.
Why can't we live always
not just putting ourselves first
but all others too, as one?

The life journey, I think,
would find all things working well,
or if broken, everyone would
work together to fix them.

Cell Phone Washing

Once more
I have allowed the washing machine
to clean my cell phone.

It no longer works.

I remember the dial days—
large black counter and wall hanging.

Times too, when operators
had to connect you to another person
and party lines made fun listening.

Everyone seemed
not to be on the phone all the time.
We had conversations face to face.

Yes, those were the good old days
and no washing machines were required.

Computer Ills

Computers, like cars,
seem now to be
one of those human tools
one can't live without.

A virus attacks again,
like the human pandemic.
The computer sick
with its own virus.

I need now to find
a skilled computer person,
a tech doctor
to save my computer.

Life goes farther and farther
away from the simple
or the easy to do.
Tomorrow, even harder, I think.

I still have my pen and paper,
the words still appear as I write.
Technology is a great thing
until it decides not to work.

A Dog's Life

Emmett the dog
seems to run now
better than me.

I'm old
but he is as old as me,
at least in dog years.

I try and keep up
as he takes the leash
clear to the end.

Even stronger,
he seems not to be breathing heavy
even after running a good distance.

I on the other hand,
gasp, trying to catch my breath.
Emmett just looks at me.

I can tell
he's wondering
why we stopped.

Nature and the Cat

The sunshine
filters through the bush's leaves.

The front casts multi-greens to my eyes,
and the back, limb patterns
made on the old alder trunk.

An east wind breeze,
known only by feel and seeing,
rakes the morning dew off the grass.

The sky
is mostly an empty blue ocean,
a promise of a good life day.

I go out into it.
The sunlight has
burned away the night.

The cool
shivers my exposed skin,
calling me to cover up.

A friend's cat
waits for food and me,
the food more important, I know.

The cat fed and happy,
I go out again into nature
and let it recapture me.

A woodpecker hugs a tree
and sends out Morse code messages
with its pecking beak.

I watch a blackbird and a robin
search here and there for breakfast.
I have to go and get some too.

Is it not a wonderful gift
that I get to see and live today?

I leave this place now,
memories taken with me,
and a few words on a page too.

A Silent Moment

Nine o'clock
on this August night
full dark has come,
and quietly, slowly, goes to silence.

These moments
seem harder to find.

I gather up silence
and put it in my memory book
so I can take it out now and then
and remember.

This silent moment was brief.
Noise came from the black.

When You Listen, You Can Hear

I sometimes stop the ticking of time,
then I sit in the quiet
and listen for the silence to come.
I heard the sunshine burn through the clouds,
the flowers bursting into color.

I heard the stream waters talking to the fish,
the owl's lost feather floating to the ground,
the smoke rising from the fire, then disappearing,
the blades of grass bending toward the sun,
and then the earth breathed.

I heard the hawk floating on the heated air,
your almost forgotten whisper passing my ears,
the dark pushing aside the light to end another day,
the stars coming out of hiding in the darkness,
and waited for the next poem's words to talk to me.

The Geese, My Father, and I Walk

The cold makes me shiver as I go through the door. I walk each day and follow wherever my feet will take me. I carry yesterday with my father in my pocket, hoping today when I stop, we will have a conversation. Then, I will continue my walk and write a song to the rhythm of my steps, and maybe try to sing it. The wind rises and swirls and the sound calls its passing through the trees. The last orange leaf of fall now leaves the tree bare.

I catch the leaf as it flies by. A small treasure to carry home with me. The geese have left me, and my eyes can see the sky, but if it's meant to be, the geese and I will walk again tomorrow.

Nature Plays

Mother Nature is playing.
Sunshine, rain, and even hail
take their turn.

Mostly, I watch from the window,
but I go out
to find coffee and a poem.

A sister's phone call
finds me too.

A good day, though
a few memories pass by
and I realize again
getting old is a good thing.

It's raining again,
it's time to go.
I'll let my face get wet.

The Snow

In its unnumbered softness,
it falls giving earth a beautiful blanket of white.
The trees bow
as they catch the whiteness.
I catch my breath from the cold,
or is it the great picture that fills my eyes?
I feel very small.
I step out and become part of the picture.
I reach out,
I watch as the snow melts in my hand,
only a moment but long enough.
I laugh and the snow falls faster.

Winter Holds On

The frozen river comes alive,
climbing onto the land's edge.

Mountains of ice
crack and break,
conversations of cold
fill the air.

The calendar says spring.
Winter only laughs at us,
cold wind and frost
telling another story.

Icy roads ditch cars,
people rush
from one warm place to another.

The sun
loses its battle to warm.

The End of the Path

As the power went off, I searched for a candle. We kept them ready in a drawer for an event such as this. I lit the candle and placed it in front of me so the dim light it cast off reached toward me and I could just see the paper on which I had been writing. The light flickered and moved in the soft flow that went across the room from the window that was slightly open. As I sat at the table in the almost dark room, a poem was given to me:

The candlelight made a path
that I was supposed to follow.

I took the first step
in the sunlight that didn't shine brightly.

I now have been on this path
for a lifetime.

The candle still burns,
even though my eyes can no longer see it.

I think I am ninety-two now,
although I don't really care about age anymore.

Today, to my surprise,
again, I found the burning candle.

It was still beautiful as it burned
and the path was still there.

Then as I watched,
the candlelight went out.

It was strange—there was still a light.
I didn't need the candle anymore.

I laid down in the silence
as I realized I had reached the end of the path.

THE PASSING OF TIME

The Passing of Time

It seems to me now
yesterdays
keep getting farther and farther away.

Memories
seem to hide
in someone else's life.

All the mirrors I look in
tell me
gray must be my favorite color.

Someone told me age
is just a state of mind,
forgetting to tell me what state I was in.

Still, how lucky am I
the sun again brought the morning
and touched my face with it.

The birds sang to the dawn.
Ocean waves called the gulls,
and your face again found my eyes.

Forgetting I Might Grow Old

A long time ago, when I was young,
I forgot I might grow old.
Now that it has happened,
I remember
why I might have forgotten.

Opening Doors

I will keep opening more doors than I close.
In this way, I think
I will be closer to finding myself again,
and if I am really lucky
I will find you behind one of them, too.

This Time I Know

Most times
I do not know.
This time I know,
yet not wanting to.

Is it a protection
that life most times
is not consumed
with death?

How would I see then
the rainbow of dawn and sunset,
the eagle floating the warm air currents,
the first breath of the newborn baby?

How would I hear
the birds' morning song,
the breeze whispering into my ears,
the heartbeat of a lover?

How would I feel
the softness of a kiss,
the touch of hand searching to be held,
the first snowflake of winter?

How would I know
the painter's painting,
the musician's song sung,
the flower's first bloom?
Or find the long-lost friend?

Yes, now death stalks him,
and maybe soon
it will be my turn to let time win.
Until then I will live, I must live.

To Teach

I was once a teacher,

After a long time,
I realized
the best thing I could teach anyone
was how to open all the doors to themselves.

So, I held a light at each door
and watched as they stepped through.

A Word

As I listened to you sing,
I realized
there are so many, many different ways
to know, to hear, to feel
a word.

Wide Open Spaces

I grew up
in a place
with no end.

I've always felt
free,
open to dream the impossible.

A small town,
one main street,
I knew all the faces.

Beyond,
only fields
that seemed not to end.

I lived outside
as much
as I could.

I found early
the good and bad
of life.

And I knew
my soul was for play
here in God's playground.

Time
has taken me
many places.

Yet my heart
still lives in those
wide open spaces.

I Find the Quiet Place

I find the quiet place
to take leave of sound,
a place where you can hear
the silence.

The journey of the day
brings a gentle song,
the sun on my back
and a moment or two alone.

I try not to hurry.
Time does that already for me,
as soon the daylight
will hide itself in the night.

A bird notices my passing.
It hardly feels my footsteps.
I will pause to let my eyes see,
then follow those who came before.

So often in life
I am lost to myself,
today I just let me be
and followed my feet along.

Want

Want gets overworked. I sometimes hope to have days of not wanting. Maybe because I'm getting older, the wanting of things has lost a lot of its appeal. Yet, there are things I want.

I want more days of this life. I want to see more of friends and family. I do want to write.

So, like most people I do want things but it's things that I now think are really important, like being with each of you here tonight. I want this more than words can say.

I have discovered that I must try and find time just for myself. I find time to go outside and see the sunrise, take a walk on the beach and listen to the waves, see if they sound different than the last time I heard them. I listen to hear a bird and try to see it. I stand out in the open and feel the breeze on my face. In the winter, as it snows, I try and catch snowflakes—they really are all different.

Gravel roads sing when you walk on them. I want to see the faces and hear the voices of ones I haven't seen in a long while—it lifts me up. I look at the paintings on people's walls, snapshots of God, I think. Music, all kinds, touches my heart and eases the hardness of the world.

Yet, the most important of any of my wants is love. There are more kinds of love than I can count and I want them all.

The People I Am

It is a puzzle that I am
with so many pieces missing
but life has given me many years
to try and find them and put me together.

I once thought I did not know
the ones I was supposed to find.
Then one day,
a friend handed me a piece—

You dropped this piece in your last lifetime.
I kept it for you
knowing we'd find each other again.
This piece, I know, goes
on the left side of your heart.
It's called love.

So many pieces of me
I still need to find
but my best friend gave me
the most important one
and the day will come
when I am made whole.

Wine and Conversation

Sitting on the deck,
a good end to the day,
wine and conversation.

Seeing far
mountaintops touch the sky,
each moment the sky changes.

Birds play chase games,
the wind gently moves the trees,
sun warms the body.

Life becomes easy,
music sings to the soul,
and nothing becomes everything.

The Path in, Just Before Dawn Time

In the just-before dawn time,
as the large snowflakes fall,
I go alone down the winding path
that will bring me to the whispering ocean.

The silence is deepest now,
just before it is awakened
by the light
of the dawn's rebirth.

My steps speak of their passing
in the gentle movement
of the dawn's rebirth.

My steps speak of their passing
in the gentle movement
of each grain of sand
that feels my walking.

A last turn in the path taken
gives me a clear hearing
of the waves singing
as they touch the shore.

The falling snowflakes
have whitened the path
and the beach now glows
as my eyes capture the scene.

I look out to the far beyond
what my eyes know but cannot see.
I paint this moment,
place the picture deep in my remembering.

Then, I turn to retrace my coming
along then slowly rising path,
back into the world I had left behind
but knowing that beach path walk.

Now, a forever part of me,
but I could never share it with you.
Only in finding it for yourself,
would you know that moment I found.

The Night and I

Only the glass holds back the dark
and keeps it from burying me in the night.

When you can't see what was there,
is it then gone?

You are left with only the remembering,
and when and if the light gives you seeing,
what you remember will be gone.

I will walk into the night
to absorb its different layers of blueness.

I will listen to hear what I cannot see
and feel the air as it passes me by.

My steps will take me to places
no one will know I have gone—
a journey with no beginning or end.

Then, the light will fuse the dark
into the birth of dawn,

and the night and I
will have only memories each other.

Day and Night

The morning eyes
found clouds and raindrops
and a short drive
to feed friends Neal and Karen's cat.

The sunset the night before
was a golden blanket
that showed itself
through light clouds and forest trees.

So much beauty given to us
if only we pause to see it.
The sunrise was hidden
but I let my mind see it.

Summer is going quickly
as flower petals begin
to ground themselves.
September time is close at hand.

I do my best now
to give each day the best of me—
more help for all and less hurt, I hope,
and try to be gentle on my journey.

The Silence of Time

The silence of time
is deafening.

We know if it's passing,
our body tells us so
without seeing another sunrise
or looking at a watch or clock.

I have seen too much of time,
as some wise young one would tell me.
I am in the autumn of my years
or maybe even the winter.

Time has grayed my hair and my hearing,
my hopes and dreams,
and my memories, too,
but not my ability to love you.

I do remember the small of myself,
the time when time didn't matter,
except it went too slow for your next birthday
or the excitement of Christmas.

The light of day again loses to the dark of night,
another signal to the no stopping of time.
I try and not be concerned about this
but the missing of you might happen too soon.

For the moment at least,

even if time says it might be my last,
I will give it over to these words,
hoping another with plenty of time will find them.

How Many Times: In Time

Time passes through my body
to tell me it has come and gone,
like the sands through an hourglass,
except I cannot turn me over
and start again.

Things called years
gather us all up.
I have enough now
to see in the mirror
that my reflection
is what my father once saw.

This life story of mine,
like many I had had before, I think,
is only one page in the novel
I am writing
that will give my soul a place to live.

How many times
I have come upon myself I cannot say,
as each life lived is kept secret
from the one before and the one after.

I watch for others too,
those who have walked with me before,
helping me remember who I was and am,
and giving me little nudges
to new pieces I should gather up.

When is my last life?
Do I get a say when it is?
The soul already knows.
It only waits for me to remember
and I will join all others in *The One*.

DAY'S END

A Quiet Place

I go to a quiet place.

I still hear the breeze,
the birds, and the babbling brook.

My footsteps fall on the path
and there is a murmur of rustling grass.

My mind lays down.
With each step
I move closer to nothing.

I wait without waiting.

I came to this place
searching for a little more of me,
knowing already
the whole of me I already have,
I only have to see me completely.

So, as I come to the end,
at least of this path taken,
the ocean speaks
with its never-ending voice.

Once More: Five River Roasters

A coffee shop,
for me,
more than a want.
It's a need.

Here, I find
people I know
and a poem or two
sent to me here.

Busy or quiet,
here I can
ease into myself
and push the rush aside.

Music floats in the air.
Hurry up takes a rest.
People here
know the coffee I drink.

Simple pleasures
many times are the best,
and you leave here
with mood and soul softened.

There are windows
here that let my eyes
escape into the distance
and see dreams come by.

But I am moving away.
Maybe there is a coffee shop
in that new town
that will have some of this place.

When I come back to visit,
I will come here again.
My pickup truck knows the way
and I'll ask for a cup of fog.

The Call of Nature

Nature whispered into my ear,
come, come, now is the time.

I rose, as if sleepwalking
through the door that was not there,
as I took myself toward the unknown.

The air was so soft that I did not feel it.
The sun had just awoken,
and had paused for a moment
on the very top of the mountain.

I followed myself into the trees
that had just begun to capture
the first of the morning light.

My steps followed no path
but seemed to know
where they were supposed to go.

I came upon a stream
flowing in slow motion
and almost unheard
from where it came
to where it was going.
I did not know
but hoped to find out.

I sat next to the stream
and told it my life story,
hoping that it would be pleased
and carry it to the last ocean,
where everything and everyone goes.

A long life lived,
and I hoped again that I would be taken
to the place I had always wanted to go.

Ocean Edge Walk

The waves here
come upon a rocky shore
splashing and erupting spouts of water,
painting a beautiful picture.

Again, I am made small
standing in front of such vastness.

Endless water only stopped
by the distant horizon,
where water and sky greet each other.

The ocean today, a charcoal gray,
its usual blue lost
in a storm-cloud cover.

The gulls protest too,
wondering when the sun will show itself.

Spring greens of bud and leaf
now recolor bare winter limbs
and capture the April breeze,
moving to the morning-earth rhythms.

Soon, I will heed the call,
erasing myself
to become part
of this world painting.

Day's End

The setting sun
colors the clouds over the ocean
as it goes over
the edge of the water.

A gentle ending
to another day,
as it eases itself
into the darkness of the night.

So, too, will I
fade into the night
in a search
for the world of dreams.

To Read the Book of Life

I made a bed
out of a thousand stars
and a pillow out of the soft white clouds
and slept with the angels.

The book of lives
was opened to the stories of me
and my becoming.

The long time
had become only moments.
The pages told of the lives
that were and will be for me.

I awake again, grounded.
What had been
was a question among many
that I knew would go unanswered.

Sometimes though,
answers are unneeded
and I feel myself
into my next life.

The pages of me
will turn to another journey
as the pieces of me
continue to fall into place.

And my place
in the all of it
will be seen and heard
with the singing of my soul.

A Lifetime Walk

I walked the miles.
The distance to nowhere
was a long way
and took beyond time.

I was never alone,
for I had taken you with me.
I could see you everywhere
except with my eyes.

My clock became the sun
and the nighttime stars
and after just a moment
my hair had turned gray.

My travels took me to many places
with long stays
in a few of them.
These I called home.

For a long time,
I hoped a corner turned
would again, as before,
bring us face to face.

Of all my memories made,
most have faded into almost forgotten.
All of them
except for you.

All my lived years
have now made me old
but I still walk
and I remember the yesterday of us.

The Journey of a Life Lived

The journey of life
finds me grappling with the embers
of my time left
before my next journey begins.

The turbulence of this one
leaves me wondering
what I will see waiting
when my last breath is taken.

Will my soul
fly through clouds of doubt
to the place of dreaming,
where the next life waits to begin?

Will this body of mine
become the loom of life on earth,
or will it swim
in the waters of the ocean?

How Did You Live?

Lay down softly on the world,
follow the path that leaves no footsteps,
give back more than you have taken,
and ready yourself at the end
for the new beginning you will be given.

A Day and a Night

Gather yourself up
place your eye upon the dawn
and give praise
you have received another one.

If the sky is blue,
swim into the heavens
until again you can touch the stars.

And if you are lucky enough to see her,
then whisper in God's ear a soft *thank you.*

Return then, just in time
to see the setting sun
kiss the clouds
with red, pink, yellow and gold.

As the last of the sunlight fades away,
hold hands with the night
and dream yourself
into the best tomorrow
you've ever lived.

In the Words: Life

The words again
kiss the end of my pen
and the words of me
flow again to paper.

Like a gentle song
being sung to me,
I hear the river of letters
and swim among them.

Soon the words and I
are one,
like little pieces of me
so those who see, know me.

The poem
tells me I am alive,
and together we touch
and are touched.

I have left myself behind,
and if these words
are read by you,
I am given life again.

Gratitude

First, I would thank my parents and brothers and sisters who were my support system in my early years. I'm also very grateful to my wife, Mary, my son Nicholas, and his wife Kelsey, for all their support and love, and of course, my grandchildren.

Next, thanks to those who read, typed, and encouraged me during my early writing.

Now, fifty years later, I still write with the support of many. Thanks I give to a few: Neal Lemery, Karen Keltz, the late Jon Dwigans, Mary Pat Eckley, Linda Shuford, Marion Grassley, Kitt Patten, Sherry Green, Deborah Hobbie, and so many others. Special thanks to Dana Cunningham Anderson for inspiring me in her workshops for all these many years, and to all the writers who participated in those workshops who inspired me as well.

Last, and most importantly, a very special thanks to Lana Hechtman Ayers who gave life to this book of poems of my words, having found enough in me to put it out in the world.

About the Author

John Wood was born in Fort Dodge, Iowa, but shortly relocated to Hermiston, Oregon with his family while his dad was still serving overseas during World War II. John was the second oldest of six children. He attended Eastern Oregon College in La Grande and earned a degree in Elementary Education. John worked his entire career as an educator at East Elementary School in Tillamook, Oregon. He spent thirty years teaching fourth, fifth, and sixth grade, then returned after retiring to be a substitute teacher for another twelve years. John met his with Mary while she was teaching third grade at the same school. Their son Nicholas is a Fire Investigator for Bureau of Land Management.

John has always been an avid reader, especially of mysteries. After retiring from teaching, he took up golf, more-or-less full-time. He's always enjoyed golf, even when the ball refuses to go straight. John started writing poetry during college in the mid nineteen-sixties. Early on, the writing was a way to examine and express his feelings, as he wasn't one to talk about them much. His writing took off once he moved to Tillamook. And after retirement, he spent many happy cups of coffee in coffee shops filling yellow legal pads with his verse. He might even have penned a few poems in bars. He continues to write anywhere he can, as often as he can. The words come to him as a gift.

John moved to Tillamook in 1970, and after over fifty years of living there, is embarking on a new adventure in Corvallis, Oregon, closer to his son Nicholas, daughter-in-law Kelsey, and two grandchildren.

www.ingramcontent.com/pod-product-compliance
Lightning Source LLC
LaVergne TN
LVHW091143080826
845145LV00008B/2234

* 9 7 8 1 9 5 6 8 2 8 0 0 9 *